The Events

by

David Greig

Commissioned by Actors Touring Company
and Drammatikkenshus, Oslo.

Co-produced by Actors Touring Company, Young Vic,
Brageteatret and Schauspielhaus Wien.

The Events premiered at the Traverse Theatre, Edinburgh
on 4th August 2013.

COMPANY

Clifford Samuel The Boy
Derbhle Crotty Claire
Magnus Gilljam Pianist

Ramin Gray Direction
John Browne Composer
Chloe Lamford Designer
Charles Balfour Lighting
Alex Caplen Sound
Polina Kalinina Associate Director
Oda Radoor Dramaturg
Brigitte Auer Dramaturg
Julia Horan Casting

Jess Banks Company Stage Manager
Jon Jewett Technical Stage Manager
Joel Price Sound Engineer

ATC would like to thank the following people
for their input into the development of
The Events:

Kai Johnsen, Oda Radoor, Dramatikkens Hus (Oslo),
all the interviewees during the Oslo research period;
Neill Quinton, Alice Chesterman and the Voicelab programme
at the South Bank Centre and all the volunteers who sang for us
at the development workshops; Obi Abili and Emma Fielding;
Dr Mark Slater; Dr. Shakti Lamba; Kathleen Bryson; Bjørn Ihler;
David Lan, Frederica Notley and the Young Vic;
National Theatre Sound Department; Chris Main and the
Clifftown Theatre, Southend; Kirsty Bushell, Amanda Drew,
Derbhle Crotty, Rona Morrison, Jack Tarlton and Caz Liske

A special thanks to all Community Choirs that took part
in the production. For a list of all the choirs that participated,
go to www.atctheatre.com

BIOGRAPHIES

Derbhle Crotty   Claire

Training: Samuel Beckett Centre, Trinity College, Dublin.

For Actors Touring Company: Crave, Illusions

Theatre includes: *Sive, The Dead, Marble, Tales of Ballycumber, An Ideal Husband, The Three Sisters, A Month in the Country, The Plough and the Stars, The Well of the Saints, The Mai* (Abbey Theatre), *Best Man* (Everyman/ Project), *Dubliners, Everyday* (Corn Exchange), *The Beauty Queen of Leenane* (Young Vic), *The Field* (Gaiety Theatre), *The Silver Tassie, The Gigli Concert* (Druid), *I'll be the Devil, Macbeth, Penelopiad, Hamlet, Camino Real, Little Eyolf* (RSC), *The Alice Trilogy, The Weir* (Royal Court Theatre), *The Home Place* (Gate Theatre, Dublin/Comedy Theatre, London), *Dancing at Lughnasa* (Gate Theatre Dublin), *Bailegangaire* (Peacock Theatre), *Summerfolk, The Merchant of Venice, The Playboy of the Western World* (National Theatre), *Sive* (Druid/ Gaiety Theatre), *The Good Father* (Druid/Project), *Portia Coughlan* (Abbey Theatre/Royal Court), *Miss Julie* (Vesuvius).

Televison and film include: *Noble* (Destiny Films), *Stella Days* (Berystede Films), *Joy* (Venom Films), *The Clinic* (RTE), *Notes on a Scandal* (Scott Rudin Productions), *Inside I'm Dancing* (Momentum), *The Merchant of Venice* (WGBH), *Any Time Now* (Nora Films Ltd), *Poorhouse* (Ocean Films), *Gold in the Streets* (RTE).

Clifford Samuel   The Boy

Training: Guildhall School of Music and Drama

Theatre includes: *Troilus and Cressida* (RSC/Wooster Group), *The Two Gentlemen of Verona, Julius Caesar, Arden of Faversham* (RSC), *Titus Andronicus, Merchant of Venice* (RSC Workshop), *Mother Courage, Statement of Regret* (National Theatre), *The Changeling* (Cheek By Jowl/Barbican), *The Lightning Child* (Globe Theatre), *One Monkey Don't Stop No Show* (Tricycle Theatre/tour), *Obama The Mamba* (Curve Leicester/The Lowry Salford), *The Girl In The Yellow Dress* (Theatre 503/Salisbury Playhouse), *Every Coin* (Soho Theatre), *In The Blood* (Finborough Theatre), *Carthage Must Be Destroyed* (Theatre Royal, Bath), *The Burial* (Almeida Theatre), *Chasing the Moment* (Arcola Theatre), *Exit Sign (*Royal Court Rough Cuts Festival), *Tierno Bokar* workshop with Peter Brook at Bouffe Du Nord, Paris.

Television and film includes: *The Lock In* (Papercutt Productions), *Betsy & Leonard* (Iron Box Films), *Looking for Jacob* (Met Films), *Sex & Drugs & Rock & Roll* (Aegis Film Fund, DJ Films, Lipsync Productions), *Shoot on Sight* (Aron Govil Productions), RTS/BAFTA award nominated *The Bill* – 3-part story, *Salvation* (as Tyrone), *Roman's Empire, London's Burning* and *Grange Hill.*

Magnus Gilljam   Pianist

Musical direction credits include: English Pocket Opera's family adaptation of Rossini's *La Cenerentola* (Cochrane Theatre/Unicorn Theatre), *The Full Monty* (New Players Theatre), *State Fair* (Trafalgar Studios), *Just So* (Tabard Theatre), *HMS Pinafore* and *The Pajama Game* (Union Theatre). For the past four years has also been musical director for the annual pantomime at Buxton Opera House. He is an associate tutor on the musical theatre programme at Guildford School of Acting (GSA).

David Greig   Writer

His award winning work includes: *The Letter of Last Resort; Fragile; The Strange Undoing of Prudencia Hart; Midsummer; Dunsinane; Damascus* and *Miniskirts of Kabul; Brewers Fayre, Outlying Island; The American Pilot; Pyrenees; The Cosmonaut's Last Message to the Woman He Once Loved in the Former Soviet Union; The Architect* and *Europe.*

Adaptations include: *Creditors, The Bacchae; Tintin in Tibet; When the Bulbul Stops Singing; Caligula; Peter Pan* and *Charlie and the Chocolate Factory.*

Work for children and young people includes: *The Monster in the Hall; Yellow Moon; Gobbo and Dr Korczak's Example.* He has also written extensively for radio.

Films include: *Vinyan* and *A Complicated Kindness;* he is working with Film Four on a screen adaptation of his stage play *Midsummer.*

Ramin Gray   Director

For ATC: *The Golden Dragon* by Roland Schimmelpfennig; *Crave* by Sarah Kane; *Illusions* by Ivan Viripaev.

Theatre in the UK includes: *The Malcontent* by John Marston, *A Message for the Broken-Hearted* and *Cat and Mouse (Sheep)* by Gregroy Motton, *The Child* by Jon Fosse, *Autumn and Winter* by Lars Noren. At the Royal Court theatre he directed *Over There* by Mark Ravenhill, *The Ugly One* and *The Stone* by Marius von Mayenburg, *Ladybird* by Vassily Sigarev, *Terrorism* by the Presnyakov Brothers, *Push Up* by Roland Schimmelpfennig, *Motortown* by Simon Stephens, *Way to Heaven* by Juan Mayorga and *Advice to Iraqi Women* by Martin Crimp. At the RSC he directed *The American Pilot* by David Greig and *I'll be the Devil* by Leo Butler.

Theatre abroad includes: *Orphans* by Dennis Kelly and *On the Shore of the Wide World* by Simon Stephens in Vienna; *Harper Regan* by Simon Stephens at the Salzburg Festival and Hamburg; *The Ugly One* by Marius von Mayenburg in Moscow.

Opera includes: *The Importance of Being Earnest* by Gerald Barry at ROH; *Bliss* by Brett Dean at Hamburgische Staatsoper; and *Death in Venice* by Benjamin Britten at Hamburgische Staatsoper and Theater an der Wien.

Ramin is currently Artistic Director of Actors Touring Company.

John Browne   Composer

Training: University College Cork with Gerald Barry and Séamas de Barra; Manhattan School of Music in New York (Fulbright Award).

Opera includes: *Babette's Feast, Demon Juice* (ROH), *Early Earth Operas, Midnight's Children* (English National Opera), *A Nightingale Sang* (Southbank Centre) and *Small Selves, Out of Suffering* (Westminster Abbey).

Films include: *The Itch of the Golden Nit.*

Other: choral arrangements for the band *Elbow.*

In the last few years he has been composer-in-residence at FNSNM, Kings College London. His music has been chosen to represent Ireland at the International Rostrum of Composers in Paris and has been performed at the Dublin Festival of Twentieth Century Music.

Chloe Lamford Designer

Designs for theatre include:_Circle Mirror Transformation_ and _Open Court_ (Royal Court Theatre), _Salt, Root and Roe_ (Donmar Warehouse/Trafalgar Studios), _Disco Pigs, Sus_, and _Blackta_ (costume designer) (Young Vic), _My Shrinking Life, Appointment with the Wicker Man, Knives in Hens_ (National Theatre Scotland), _Praxis Makes Perfect, The Radicalisation of Bradley Manning_ (National Theatre Wales), _Boys_ (Headlong Theatre), _Cannibals_ and _The Gate Keeper_ (Manchester Royal Exchange), _My Romantic History, The History Boys_ (Sheffield Crucible), _Ghost Story_ (Sky Arts Live Drama), _Britannicus_ (Wilton's Music Hall), _Joseph K, The Kreutzer Sonata_ (Gate Theatre), _It Felt Empty..._ (Clean Break), _Everything Must Go!_ and _This Wide Night_ (Soho Theatre), _The Mother Ship, How to Tell the Monsters from the Misfits_ (Birmingham Rep), _The Country_ (Salisbury Playhouse), _Desire Lines_ (Sherman, Cardiff), _Small Miracle_ (Tricycle/ Mercury Colchester) -Winner Best Design TMA awards, 2007.

Designs for opera include:_The Little Sweep_ and _Let's Make An Opera_ (Malmo Opera House, Sweden), _The Magic Flute_ (English Touring Opera), _War and Peace_ (Scottish Opera/ RCS), _Cunning Little Vixen, Orpheus in the Underworld_ (Royal College of Music), _La Calisto_ (Early Opera Company).

Charles Balfour Lighting

For ATC: _Crave, Illusions._

Theatre includes: _Marilyn_ (Citizens Theatre), _Who's Afraid of Virginia Woolf_ (Sheffield Crucible, Northern Stage), _Beauty Queen of Leenane_ (Young Vic), _Now or Later, The Girlfriend Experience, The Ugly One_ (Royal Court), _I''ll Be the Devil_ (RSC), _Loot_ (Tricycle Theatre), _Christmas Carol_ (Kingston Swan), _The Weir_ (Octagon, Bolton), _Angels in America, The English Game_ (Headlong), _The Duchess of Malfi, Hedda Gabler, Don Quixote_ (West Yorkshire Playhouse), _A Doll's House, Christmas Carol, Son of Man_ (Northern Stage), _The Flint Street Nativity, The Tempest_ (Liverpool Playhouse), _Cleansed_ (Oxford Stage Company), _Hair, Woyzeck, Witness_ (Gate Theatre), _Amadeus, Masterclass_ (Derby Playhouse), _Baby Doll, Therese Raquin, Bash_ (Citizens Glasgow), _Through the Leaves_ (Southwark Playhouse / Duchess West End).

Dance includes: 26 works for Richard Alston Dance Company (Sadler's Wells & worldwide), _Red Balloon_ (Royal Opera House for Aletta Collins; _Dance Cross_ (Beijing Dance Academy), _Lap Dancer, Bloom_ (Aletta Collins/Rambert Dance Company), _Eden/Eden_ (Wayne McGregor/San Francisco Ballet/Stuttgart Ballet), _Four Seasons_ (Oliver Hindle/Birmingham Royal Ballet), _White, Women in Memory_ (Rosemary Butcher/Tate Modern Turbine Hall & across Europe) and many others.

Music includes: _Opera Shots_ by Orlando Gough, Nitin Sawhney & Jocelyn Pool (ROH), _Carmen, Werther_ (Opera North), _Confucious Says HMDT_(Hackney Empire - winner of the Royal Philharmonic Prize for new work), _Saul_ (Opera North), _The Birds_ (The Opera Group), _Jordan Town_ (Errollyn Wallen – ROH), _Writing to Vermeer_ (London Sinfonietta, QEH), _Thimble Rigging_ (Scott Walker /Meltdown – Royal Festival Hall), Zbigniew Preisner's _Silence, Night and Dreams (_Acropolis, Athens).

Alex Caplen   Sound

For ATC: *Crave, Illusions, The Golden Dragon.*

Theatre sound design credits include: *Carpe Diem* (National Theatre – New Views), *A Time to Reap, Ding Dong the Wicked, Goodbye to All That, Wanderlust* (Royal Court), *Over There* (Royal Court Theatre & Schaubühne Berlin), *Constellations* (Associate - Duke of York's), *Ogres* (Tristan Bates), *It's About Time* (Nabokov), *Mine, Ten Tiny Toes, War and Peace* (Shared Experience), *Stephen and the Sexy Partridge* (Old Red Lion/Trafalgar Studios) *Peter Pan, Holes, Duck Variations* (UK Tour), *The Wizard of Oz, The Entertainer* (Nuffield Theatre), *Imogen* (Oval House/Tour).

Opera includes: *The Love for Three Oranges, Tosca* (Grange Park Opera).

As Sound Operator/Engineer: *Edinburgh Military Tattoo 2009 - 2012; Bronte, Kindertransport* (Shared Experience), *Blood Brothers* (UK Tour), *Ballroom* (UK tour). Other work includes large-scale international music touring as a Front of House mix engineer.

Alex is a Senior Sound Technician at The National Theatre and an Associate Artist (Sound) for ATC.

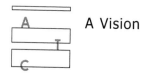

A Vision

'ATC produces work that inspires me to reconsider what a play can be and what theatre can do. Magical.'

Simon Stephens, Olivier award-winning playwright

In an increasingly globalised age, where society and identity is in constant flux, the need for art that rediscovers our sense of self and our relations with others is at its strongest.

ATC fulfils this need by touring international contemporary theatre. Our mission is to take daring and curious new work further and further afield, and we want you to go with us there.

A Company

Ramin Gray   Artistic Director
Nick Williams   Executive Director
Ania Obolewicz   Assistant Producer
Polina Kalinina   Trainee Associate Director
Tiru Thiruvilangam   Development and Audiences Manager
Ed Armitage   Finance Manager

David Burns PR   Press
david@davidburnspr.com / 07789 75408

The Board at Actors Touring Company is:

Caroline Bailey
Professor Maria Delgado   Chair
Nelson Fernandez OBE
Caroline Firstbrook
David Massarella
Vincent Keaveny
Michael Quine
Hetty Shand

ATC is a registered charity No. 279458

Supported using public funding by
ARTS COUNCIL ENGLAND

An Opportunity

'The Actors Touring Company's passion and enthusiasm for the wilder reaches of contemporary international theatre has always seemed exemplary to me. They have long been an outfit doggedly devoted to sharing gems from around the world with British audiences. I urge you to support them in any way you can.

Richard Wilson OBE, director and broadcaster

ATC wants you to be a part of its plans by becoming an ATC Patron and making a gift that will have a significant impact on our work. As a Patron, you will receive:

- Invitations to ATC performances and open rehearsals as well as other special events throughout the year.
- One-to one meetings with Ramin Gray, Artistic Director, to discuss current projects and future plans.
- Dedication on ATC's website, programmes, and play-texts.
- The Patrons e-newsletter, sent quarterly, containing exclusive behind-the-scenes news and interviews with ATC's travelling troupe of theatre-makers.
- Opportunities to meet artists, writers and actors from all over the world.

To find out how to take part, email atc@atctheatre.com

A Journey

ATC is on a voyage and we thank the following supporters for helping us get this far:

Caroline Bailey, Gianni Botsford and Anahi Copponex, Jo Cottrell, Stuart Cox, Professor Maria Delgado, Cas and Philip Donald, Conor Fenton, Nelson Fernandez OBE, Caroline Firstbrook and Ian Smith, Veronica Gledhill Hall, Andrew Hochhauser QC, Kent Lawson and Carol Tambor, David Lubin and Tamara Joffe, Rich Major, David Massarella, Neil and Elena Pearse, Michael Quine, and Jon and NoraLee Sedmak.

We also thank the following trusts and foundations for their kind support of our work:

Bermondsey Metals, Boris Karloff Foundation, British Council, Chalmers Engineering, D'Oyly Carte Charitable Trust, Fidelio Trust, Garrick Charitable Trust, Genesis Foundation, Iran Heritage Foundation, Royal Victoria Hall, Foundation, Sylvia Waddilove Foundation, Thistle Trust, and Unity Theatre Trust.

Follow the journey: atctheatre.com
facebook.com/actorstouringcompany   twitter.com/ATCLondon

The Events

By David Greig

Touring in Buskerud, Norway spring 2014.

In 2014 Norway celebrates the 200th anniversary of our nation's constitution. Brageteatret would like to use this celebration to question and comment on the state of the modern Norwegian society, through a variety of projects and different perspectives.

The Events will be part of Brageteatret's program of celebration, will tour in Buskerud and collaborate with local choirs in local venues during the spring of 2014. The theme of *The Events* draws attention to an international phenomenon which has also deeply affected Norway. It is important to us as a Norwegian theatre to explore this phenomenon, and through the international collaboration on *The Events* we can do from a distance. With David Greig's new text and the ATC's interpretation of it, we can get a different perspective on some of the challenges our modern society faces.

Premiere Brageteatret - Drammen March 2014

BRAGETEATRET was established in 2000 and is a professional theatre and a Public Organization, owned by Buskerud County and Drammen City. The theatre receives funding from the two owners together with the Norwegian state who is the main funder. BRAGETEATRET is a touring theatre that produces performances for all age groups. BRAGETEATRET values and invests in new writing for the stage, because we regard this as the future of theatre.

The Events
Die Ereignisse

An Actors Touring Company, Brageteatret, Schauspielhaus Wien & Young Vic Theatre Co-Production

by David Greig
German by Brigitte Auer
Director: Ramin Gray
Cast Vienna: Franziska Hackl, Florian von Manteuffel

Do not miss the
first German-language production of
The Events: Die Ereignisse!

Premiere: November 22nd, 2013,
Schauspielhaus Wien

Schauspielhaus Vienna is like no other German language theatre a theatre of the present. The programming of this unique stage concentrates exclusively on contemporary writing. The motto of season 2013/14 will be "100 Jahre Wahn&Sinn" (100 Years of Madness) and will focus on a close examination of the past 100 years from a contemporary perspective.

Schauspielhaus Wien
Porzellangasse 19
1090 Vienna
Austria
Tickets: +43-1-317 01 01 18 or
karten@schauspielhaus.at

Young Vic

> 'The best theatre in London.' *Daily Telegraph*
>
> 'The Young Vic is one of our great producing theatres.'
> *The Independent*
>
> 'A powerhouse of endearing delight and shattering drama.'
> *Daily Telegraph*

We present the widest variety of classics, new plays, forgotten works and music theatre. We tour and co-produce extensively within the UK and internationally.

Our artists
Our shows are created by some of the world's great theatre people alongside the most adventurous of the younger generation. This fusion makes the Young Vic one of the most exciting theatres in the world.

Our audience
... is famously the youngest and most diverse in London. We encourage those who don't think theatre is 'for them' to make it part of their lives. We give 10% of our tickets to schools and neighbours irrespective of box office demand, and keep prices low.

Our partners near at hand
Each year we engage with 10,000 local people – individuals and groups of all kinds including schools and colleges – by exploring theatre on and off stage. From time to time we invite our neighbours to appear on our stage alongside professionals.

Our partners further away
By co-producing with leading theatre, opera, and dance companies from around the world we create shows neither partner could achieve alone.

David Lan Artistic Director
Lucy Woollatt Executive Director

The Young Vic is a company limited by guarantee, registered in England No. 1188209.
VAT registration No. 236 673 348
The Young Vic (registered charity number 268876) receives public funding from:

Lead sponsor of the Young Vic's funded ticket scheme

Get more from the Young Vic online

Sign up to receive email updates at youngvic.org/register

 youngvictheatre

 youngviclondon

 @youngvictheatre

 youngviclondon.wordpress.com

DIRECTOR'S NOTE

Every act of theatre revolves around a transaction between two communities: the performers onstage and the improvised community that constitute what we call an audience. When Anders Breivik killed 77 people in Norway in July 2011, his actions set out to destroy one community while simultaneously and unintentionally galvanising other communities around the world. From simple outpourings of grief, through reams of testimony, heated debate, lengthy judicial process, psychiatric analysis and raw soul-searching to the writing and performing of this play, it's clear that we need to churn over such events in an effort to understand. And, of course, the very best forum for those efforts remains the public, shared space of the theatre. But could it just be, as David Greig suggests, that some things remain beyond the realm of the comprehensible?

As an international touring company in a world where everyone seems to be on the move (something that Breivik clearly found deeply disturbing), this felt like an important subject for us to investigate. Sadly, since then both the Boston bombing and the events in Woolwich have kept the material resonating. In the play, David's fictional Boy crystallises so many of the dissociated young men who seem to perpetrate these events, while Claire's obsessive need for understanding seems to mirror us, the audience and our communal drive for closure.

Many plays, from the Chorus of Old Men in the *Oresteia* onwards, have found ways of embodying community on stage, underscoring the central role of theatre in civic life. The Actors Touring Company constantly arrives in different cities, performing for a few nights, then moving on. In conceiving this new play with David, I wanted to make sure we connect more deeply with audiences and find a way of representing them accurately. Hence our idea of inviting local choirs wherever we play to join us on stage each night to experience at first hand the struggle to digest but also to embody what is at stake. We are profoundly grateful to all the choirs who have developed and participated in the production of this play.

I also need to give thanks to our Norwegian collaborators and supporters – Kai Johnsen and Oda Radoor (then of Dramatikkenshus) who allowed us to gain first-hand insight into a stunned community in the wake of 22 July 2011. Since then we are pleased to have found in Elsa Aanensen and Brageteatret a Norwegian touring company who share many of our goals. We are equally blessed with our Austrian partners at Schauspielhaus Wien (Andreas Beck and Brigitte Auer) and of course with David Lan and his team at the Young Vic.

RAMIN GRAY
London, July 2013

The Events

David Greig was born in Edinburgh. His plays include *Europe*, *The Architect*, *The Speculator*, *The Cosmonaut's Last Message to the Woman He Once Loved in the Former Soviet Union*, *Outlying Islands*, *San Diego*, *Pyrenees*, *The American Pilot*, *Yellow Moon: The Ballad of Leila and Lee*, *Damascus*, *Midsummer* (*a Play with Songs*), *Dunsinane*, *The Strange Undoing of Prudencia Hart* and *The Monster in the Hall*. In 1990 he co-founded Suspect Culture to produce collaborative, experimental theatre work. His translations and adaptations include Camus's *Caligula*, Euripides' *The Bacchae*, Strindberg's *Creditors*, *Peter Pan* and *Charlie and the Chocolate Factory*.

DAVID GREIG

The Events

ff

FABER & FABER

First published in 2013
by Faber and Faber Limited
74–77 Great Russell Street, London WC1B 3DA

Reprinted with revisions 2014

Typeset by Country Setting, Kingsdown, Kent CT14 8ES
Printed in England by CPI Group (UK) Ltd, Croydon, Surrey CRO 4YY

A CIP record for this book
is available from the British Library

ISBN 978-0-571-31105-7

4 6 8 10 9 7 5 3

The Events, in a co-production by the Actors Touring Company, the Young Vic, Brageteatret and Schauspielhaus Wien, was first performed at the Traverse Theatre, Edinburgh, on 4 August 2013. The cast was as follows:

The Boy Rudi Dharmalingam
Claire Neve McIntosh

Director Ramin Gray
Assistant Director Polina Kalinina
Composer John Browne
Designer Chloe Lamford
Lighting Charles Balfour
Sound Alex Caplen

The production was revived for a new tour in June 2014, including a run at the Young Vic, London, that opened on 8 July, with the following changes of cast:

The Boy Clifford Samuel
Claire Derbhle Crotty
Pianist Magnus Gilljam

I would like to thank the following people
who helped me make the text of this play:

Oda Radoor, Franziska Hackl, Florian von Manteuffel,
Heidi Gjermundsen Broch, Brigitte Auer, John Browne,
Polina Kalinina, Jess Banks, Ramin Gray, Neve McIntosh,
Rudi Dharmalingam, Bjorn Ihler.

As usual, the best thoughts belong to them.
Any faults in the play's making are mine not theirs.

Characters

Claire

The Boy

A Choir

Repetiteur

Setting

The play takes place in a room,
the sort of place in which a choir might rehearse.

There is an urn.

A Note on the Choir

Dialogue in italic is intended for the choir.

The choir's own song should be bright and bold,
and it should offer a strong sense of the choir's identity.
It should be typical of their repertoire and not exceptional.
Its job is simply to allow them to introduce themselves
and to get the evening off to a good start.

The boy's favourite song is a production choice.

THE EVENTS

'This thing of darkness I acknowledge mine'
The Tempest

The Choir sing their own song.

*

The Boy rocks on the balls of his feet.

Claire welcomes him.

Claire Hi.
  Come in.
  Don't be shy.
  Everyone's welcome here.
  What's your name?

OK – that's OK.
  No worries at all.

You can help me put out chairs if you like?

Do you speak English?

Not to worry.
  We're all a big crazy tribe here.

Right, why don't we sing the Norwegian Coffee Song?
  Can I have you in two groups round the piano?

Why don't you join us?
  If you feel like singing – sing.
  And if you don't feel like singing.
  Well that's OK too.
  Nobody feels like singing all the time.
  Ha ha.

The Choir sing the Norwegian Coffee Song.

Claire leads the choir in call and response, finally picking the Boy, who does not join in.

> *Hente brenne knus se koke kaffien (× 2)*
> *Og sa henter viden, og sa Brenner viden*
> *Hente brenne knus se koke kaffien*
> *En kopp til, ja takk (× 4)*

*

The Boy Imagine a boy –

An aboriginal boy –

He's standing on the rocks above the Illawarra River just at the very moment three ships from England come sailing up the long grey waters of the cove.

. . .

Huge white sails –

. . .

These are craft unlike any he's ever seen – spacecraft almost –

. . .

And on these ships are convicts; a condition of personhood the boy does not know; on these ships are officers and ratings; conditions of personhood the boy does not know.

Carried on these ships are class and religion and disease and a multitude of other instruments of objectification and violence all of which are about to be unleashed upon his people.

. . .

But the boy doesn't know this yet, he doesn't know any of this yet.

. . .

The only things he knows are his land, his tribe, and the tribes beside.

. . .

And now these sails.

. . .

If you could go back in time and speak to that boy, what would you say?

You would stand on the rocks and you would point at the ships and you would say – 'Kill them. Kill them all.'

*

Claire I've taken up smoking again.

Sometimes I surprise the old men at the community centre by taking their tobacco pouch from them and saying – for fuck's sake – I'll say – for fuck's sake, you don't roll a cigarette like that, you roll a cigarette like this. And I roll it for them. Thin and tight, with barely a strand of tobacco through it.

'That's how you roll a fucking fag,' I say.

Then I light it.

And then I smoke it.

The Boy What were you like before, Claire?

Claire Before?

Before I was good.

Before we were happy.

'We' is me and Catriona –
    Catriona is my partner.
    She makes yurts.

Was my partner – is – I don't know –
    Is, I think. – Is.

We lived in a cottage by the sea. Behind the cottage was The Den: old woods on a hill. We gathered mushrooms and blueberries, you know, and wild garlic.

All wild things.

I ran a choir.

At the community centre, it's attached to the church. I ran a choir that brought together vulnerable people, old people, asylum-seekers, immigrant men, young mums and so on – it was a – the idea was – you can imagine.

We sang.

The Boy Do you pray?

Claire Yes.

The Boy And?

Claire Nothing.

The Boy Given the circumstances – perhaps –

Claire I would have thought that given the circumstances I would be positively entitled to a visit from God. I would have though the least I could expect is he would make an appearance. Wouldn't you?

What sort of circumstances do you think he might be waiting for?

Genocide?

The Boy He's here.

Claire I believe you.

Thousands wouldn't.

The Boy Nothing about faith is easy, Claire. You know that.

Events test us.

Claire Can I tell you something in confidence?

The Boy Of course.

Claire Something I haven't told anyone. Mainly because I haven't been able to put it into words. Or at least, I can put it into words but the words I would have to put it into are words that people might think sound weird, or mad.

The Boy What sort of words?

Claire Spiritual words.

The Boy What sort of spiritual words might people think it weird or mad for a priest to use?

Claire Words like 'soul'.

The Boy You think it would be weird or mad for a priest to use the word 'soul'.

Claire When I was hiding in the music room –

The Boy Yes.

Claire And the boy burst in –

And I knew I was going to die.

The Boy Yes.

Claire At that moment I felt something.

A feeling I've never had before, a feeling of tearing, of something pulling away from its moorings suddenly and in its wake – an overwhelming absence.

It was a feeling as precise and as physical as any feeling I've ever had.

And the moment I felt it, I knew what it was.

The Boy What was it?

Claire It was my soul leaving my body.

The Boy . . .

Claire . . .

The Boy When did your soul come back?

Claire It hasn't.

The Boy . . .

You're still a priest, Claire.

You have a community.

Eventually you will have to rejoin the world.

Don't you think?

Claire?

Claire At Isaac's funeral the hymn was 'How Great Thou Art'.

The first chords played
   I opened my mouth
   And

Claire Was it Isaac or was it Jesse?

Isaac?

I forget.

*

The Boy skips.

The Boy I have been thinking I might go berserk.

Viking warrior shamen were considered to be invincible because they fought their battles in an altered or 'berserking' state. To become berserk the warrior would go to a cave in the woods. There he would fast for three days. He would commune with his spirit familiar – usually a wolf or a bear. He would copy the animal's movement and embody its being. Then, when he was spiritually and physically ready, he would ingest fly agaric mushroom extract usually by drinking the urine of a reindeer stag. The warrior would fall unconscious. In his sleep he would twitch and buck and vomit. Then, finally, he would awaken. Filled with an awesome sense of his own power and strength he would march out of the forest and back down the mountain singing out his special berserker song, a song designed to induce in him his killing rage.

He would march down the mountain like the coming of thunder until at last he reached the hall of his enemy just at the moment when his enemy's people were at feast.

He would enter the hall.

He would raise his axe.

And he would go berserk.

Look at us.

All I can see about me is weakness, fear and ruined skin.

Softness.

The best thing that could happen in this world would be the coming of a great conjuring flame. A conjuring flame to sweep clean our estates and our high streets and to roar through our shops and offices burning us all at our workstations.

By the time he was my age Jesus had founded a world religion.

By the time he was my age Bob Geldof had saved Africa.

By the time he was my age Gavrilo Princip had fired the shot that started World War One.

If I'm going to make a mark on the world I have to do it now.

The only means I have are art or violence.

And I was never any good at drawing.

*

Claire screams.

The Boy Jesus.
   Mrs.
   I didn't see you.
   Fuck, sorry,
   Flip!

Claire It's OK, it was my fault.

I was – somewhere else. I'm sorry.

The Boy Jesus. You need to watch yourself, love.

Claire Yes.
   Yes.
   Sorry.

*

The Boy Frequently asked questions!

   The Choir ask the Boy questions.

Choir What's your favourite song?

My favourite song is 'Bonkers' by Dizzee Rascal!

Choir Being a tribal warrior must involve long periods of time on your own. How do you cope with the loneliness?

Choir It's difficult, there's no question of that, but it's in the nature of being a visionary that – to a certain extent – one has no peers. I guess the answer is – it's hard, but – one grows a skin.

Choir Do you have a spirit familiar?

My spirit familiar is a fox.

Choir What's your favourite film?

Lord of The Rings Part Two.

Choir What do you do when you're not involved in tribal warrior work?

I play *Call of Duty.*

Choir Do you drink?

No.

Choir Do you take drugs?

No.

Choir Are you a virgin?

No.

Choir Are you gay?

No.

Choir Do you hate foreigners?

I'm glad you asked that question. I don't hate foreigners. I hate foreigners being here. There is a difference.

Choir Do you believe in an afterlife?

Only in the sense that I expect to be etched into the neural circuitry of the minds I encounter in life – and I intend to be etched into a lot of minds. LOL!

Seriously though, I think my ideas are my afterlife.

Choir You must have to be fit to be a tribal warrior? Do you follow a special diet?

Yes! I follow the Palaeolithic diet. As described in the *Sunday Times* Lifestyle Supplement. 'Meat, green vegetables and leaves. No legumes! No grains! One eats as Stone Age man ate. I am on day three. Feeling good on it. Feeling fucking great on it actually –

Choir Your actions will be shocking to many people, many people will ask – why do you kill? What will be your answer to such persons?

I kill to protect my tribe.

Claire Really?

The Boy I kill to protect my tribe from softness.

Claire Softness?

The Boy A softness born of cheap togetherness – which is an illusion fostered by failed elites who cling on to power and wealth through immigrant labour and globalisation.

I don't know why you even read this shit, Claire.

Claire 'Blood makes the land fertile.'
'Blood must be shed in defence of the tribe.'

The Boy Switch it off.

Claire I just want to read a little more.

The Boy Do you want a cup of tea?

Claire I'm fine.

The Boy Only you must have spilled that one.

Claire Did I?

The Boy Do you want me to mop it up?

Claire It's fine.

The Boy In case it stains.

Claire Blood must be shed in defence of the tribe.

Who does he mean?

Who are the tribe?

Picts?

Angles?

Jutes?

Neanderthals?

The Boy Nobody knows.

Claire He does.

The Boy Does it matter?

Claire Of course it matters.

The Boy Why?

Claire For fuck's sake, Catriona.

It matters because I don't understand him.

How can I hate him if I don't understand him?

Sorry.

The Boy You're bound to feel –

Claire I'm fine, all right? I'm fucking fine. Stop creeping about. Stop not mopping up messes. Just leave it to stain, all right? Just stop.

The Boy Sorry.

Claire No, I'm sorry.

The Boy Claire.

On the way home, I noticed people gathering.
    Down at the promenade.
    Flowers, singing, lamps.
    I stayed for a bit.
    The atmosphere. It's surprising.
    The emotion.
    The love.
    Genuine love.

Claire For who?

The Boy I don't know exactly.

You.

The Boy Come down to the promenade with me.
  Be with the people.
  Come.

Claire It's not love.

The Boy Claire.

Claire It's not love.
  It's sentiment.
  If it were love,
  It would be for him.

*

Claire listens to 'Bonkers', by Dizzee Rascal.

*

The Boy You stole a Twix.

Claire I didn't steal it.

The Boy You walked out without paying.

Claire There was no one there.

The Boy There was a scanner.

Claire Exactly. A machine.
  A great big electronic box.

What am I supposed to do with that?

The Boy There was an assistant.

Claire So.

The Boy You could have asked for help.

Claire I did.

'What am I supposed to do with this?' I said. 'Where am I supposed to put my money? I only want a Twix.'

'Do you need help?' she said.

'Look at me,' I said. 'What am I? An animal? A bucket of meat at a metal trough? A cow? Am I cow? Is that what I am? Easing myself slowly through the abattoir? Mooing towards my own erasure?'

'Yes,' I said. 'Yes, I need fucking help.'

The Boy That's quite an angry way of asking for help, isn't it, Claire?

Claire Is it? I don't think it is.

The Boy Pushing people is quite an angry thing to do.

Claire I didn't push her.

The Boy You walked out without paying.

Claire Why should I acknowledge someone who can't even be bothered to exist?

The Boy What I really want to know, Claire, is –

Claire You're a psychologist, aren't you?
    What I really want to know is, is he mad?

The Boy Who?

Claire The boy.

The Boy Would that be important, Claire?

Claire Of course.

The Boy Why?

Claire Because if he's mad then it wasn't his fault.

Was it?

The Boy Whose fault was it?

Claire Nature's.

Like cancer.

Anyone could get cancer.

The Boy But if he's sane?

Claire Then he must be evil.

The Boy We would probably prefer to say 'empathy impaired'.

Claire What does that mean?

The Boy When someone shows lack of empathy we can clearly say that they have deviated from the human norm. If you tell me that a person has deliberately planned to cause pain to a large number of people. I can say, with confidence, that person's behaviour is empathy impaired.

Claire When I was in the music room.
   Hiding with Mrs Singh.
   We heard footsteps.
   Mrs Singh was so afraid she screamed.
   He kicked the door open and he found us.
   And then he said –

I have one bullet.
   There are two of you –
   Which one of you do you want me to shoot?
   . . .
   Which one of you do you want me to shoot?

The Boy Cruel.

Claire His empathy was not impaired when he asked that question.

When he asked that question he knew exactly how we felt.

The Boy To understand him properly, we would need to interview him.

To explore his family background.
Without that all we have is speculation.

Claire Is he mad or is he evil?

In the meantime,

What we really need to think about, Claire, is you.

Claire I'm fine.

The Boy I'm just wondering if you might be angry?

Claire I'm not angry.

The Boy Are you sure?

. . .

I got the fucking Twix, didn't I?

The Boy Because you're the person who's here, Claire.

How can we understand what happened to you?

Claire I don't want to understand what happened to me,

I know what happened to me.

I want to understand what happened to him.

*

The Choir sing 'Bonkers' by Dizzee Rascal.

Claire The father.

The Boy I just thought he was probably gay.

Claire Gay?

The Boy Not gay, as such, not actually gay –

Just massively afraid of his own homoerotic feelings.

Going to the gym, the obsession with militaria, idolisation of hard-bodied men. All his talk about sexual continence.

Masculinity in crisis.

. . .

I thought it was laughable.

I told him as much.

Claire You told him?

The Boy Over dinner.

About a year ago, I think it was his birthday.

We went to some place or other.

He wore camouflage. Frankly I thought he looked a sight but we ate. I paid. We talked.

I said, 'You should get yourself a boyfriend.'

Claire How did he take that?

The Boy I don't remember.

Claire You said to your son he should get himself a boyfriend and you don't remember what he said back?

The Boy I was drinking at the time. I don't remember very much. Most of what I remember from that time comes from what the newspapers dig up.

I find it difficult. You can imagine.

Claire Not as difficult as it is for me.

The Boy I suppose.

Although – you know – in a way, you are a victim – so people are nice to you.

People are pretty horrible to me.

Claire Do people know who you are?

The Boy Everyone.

Claire Why don't you move away?

The Boy He's my son.

Not moving away seems the least I can do.

Claire Have you been to the house?

The Boy Not since.

Claire Not since?

The Boy Not before either.

Claire You never visited him?

The Boy He lived there with his mother.

Claire I went there.

The Boy What's it like?

Claire It's not very nice.

It's on the edge of an estate in a cul-de-sac.

Broken glass, sea at the end of the street.

There were boards over the windows.

On one of the boards someone had sprayed
'CUNT'.

In red letters, three foot tall,

'Cunt.'

Did that mean him, do you think?

Or his mother?

Or you?

The Boy Maybe it didn't refer to anyone at all?

Look – I want to help you, Claire.

If anyone wants to understand what happened to him, it's me, so if you find any answers let me know because I'll tell you what: it bewilders me. The sheer horror, the scale, the nihilism, where it came from, it bewilders me –

Claire Tell me about his mother?

The Boy His mother killed herself when he was fifteen.

Claire The journalist.

Tell me about Ibn Khaldun.

The Boy Oh dear God, not this again.

Claire The boy quoted you on Ibn Khaldun.

The Boy Look, I wrote a book – a semi-humorous book intended largely to be read whilst on the lavatory – in which I expressed a perfectly valid set of questions about the decadence of contemporary society – couched in a flippant philosophical aside – and now my name is mud – I mean the whole thing's a nightmare.

Claire (*reads*) 'Old Man Moaning'.

'Ibn Khaldun knew a thing or two about moaning. This medieval Arab philosopher was a prototype grumpy old man. He had a theory that history is an endless fight between the foppish dandies of the city and the hard-bodied sheikhs of the desert. Old Ibn spotted that when cities become wealthy their wealth makes them decadent and so eventually a horde of barbarian tribesmen comes roaring out of the desert on horseback, to conquer it. Purification by blood. Civilisation renews itself. But then, what happens? The tribesmen become city dwellers of course, get wealthy and soft and soon they too hear trumpets and drums, the conjuring flame comes over the dunes to purify the city once more.'

The conjuring flame.

The Boy Yes.

Claire Which he read in your book.

The Boy With reference to my desire it should come down and consume the people who make reality television.

Not choirs.

Look –

It all comes down to which side you're on.

Claire Which side are you on?

The Boy Me?

I'm on the city walls with the poofs and the theatricals.

Claire Where's he?

The Boy He's out there.

Wandering through the blasted waste of modern life desperately searching for something he can hold on to.

Certainty.

Claire A father.

The Boy Maybe.

Claire The friend.

You know him.

The Boy I don't *know* him, *knew* him. *Knew*. I was at school with him but I wasn't his friend.

Claire OK.

The Boy It's just the newspapers keep saying I was his friend. I wasn't his friend.

Claire But you knew him.

The Boy I knew him because we were both unpopular.

During break times we would hide behind the science block lavatories to avoid getting beaten up.

We tended each other, that's all.

We weren't close, we were in proximity.

Claire Tended?

The Boy He would get hit.

Mostly we just – hung out, talked.

Claire What did you talk about?

The Boy Girls – the army – types of car –

PlayStation.

Claire Why was he unpopular?

The Boy Because he was weak.

Claire Weak?

The Boy Mentally – he was a bit breakable, you know?

Claire People picked on him because he was breakable?

The Boy Yes.

Claire That's awful.

The Boy Are you surprised?

Claire Yes?

The Boy You must have been popular.

Popular kids always think people are basically good. But that's not true. People are basically not good.

But when you're an unpopular kid at school you get left with a very particular view of humanity. Jaundiced, you might say.

Claire It's depressing.

The Boy I don't think so. I think it's actually quite liberating.

The standards one feels one has to live up to.

They're quite low.

Claire Right, could you all come and sit down?

Let's sing 'How Great Thou Art'.

*

The Choir sing. 'How Great Thou Art'.

Choir
> *O Lord my God, When I in awesome wonder,*
> *Consider all the worlds Thy hands have made;*
> *I see the stars, I hear the rolling thunder,*
> *Thy power throughout the universe displayed.*

Claire Can we stop there, could we try just humming?

The Choir hum.

> *O Lord my God, When I in awesome wonder,*
> *Consider all the worlds Thy hands have made –*

Claire Just the ladies.

Hum.

> *I see the stars, I hear the rolling thunder,*
> *Thy power throughout the universe displayed.*

Claire And now all in for the chorus.

> *Then sings my soul, my Saviour God, to Thee,*
> *How great Thou art, how great Thou art.*
> *Then sings my soul, my Saviour God, to Thee,*
> *How great Thou art, how great Thou art!*

*

Claire The politician.

I want to talk about his ideology.

The Boy You think he had an ideology?

Claire Don't you?

The Boy No.

Claire He professed an ideology.

The Boy So?

Claire Your ideology.

The Boy I know, but we absolutely reject him.

Claire I know but –

The Boy Unambiguously.

Claire He was a member of your party.

The Boy Anyone can be a member of our party.

Claire As long as you're white.

The Boy We have members who are black.

Claire Not many.

The Boy He joined our party four months before the events. He'd already decided what he was going to do by that point – didn't you read the blog?

Claire He's very enthusiastic about you in the blog.

The Boy If I knew what he was planning I'd have discouraged him.

Claire Discouraged?

The Boy Stopped.

Do you mind?

The Boy checks his phone.

I might need to pick up my girl from the nursery.

Claire How long do you have?

The Boy It's OK. I still have a few minutes.

The Boy checks his phone.

The boy's actions have been a disaster for us.

Claire Why?

The Boy He's a madman.

Claire A madman who believes the things you believe.

The Boy Exactly, so by association we appear mad or extreme.

Claire But you are extreme?

The Boy I don't think so.

I think most people deep down would agree with our ideas.

Claire You think most people are racist?

The Boy If racist means believing people are happiest, and most secure, when they live amongst their own kind, then yes. I think most people are racist, don't you?

Claire I like encountering different people. I enjoy it.

The Boy You enjoy exoticism as long as you feel in a dominant position. As long as your tribe are in control. Then it's fun, a hobby. If you felt genuine competition for housing, or resources, or jobs . . . like most people do . . . you would feel differently. It's not so easy to be open to others when your tribe feels weak.

Claire Do you feel weak?

The Boy I'm sorry – I just – I'm anxious about the buses. I don't want to miss her.

The Boy checks his phone.

Claire Maybe you should go.

The Boy No, it's OK. I have two minutes.

Claire Tell me why you think it's OK to be racist.

The Boy Look, our country is under threat.

Claire Really?

The Boy Yes.

The values we live by are under threat, our heritage, our traditions.

That might mean nothing to you but it means everything to me.

And I'm prepared to fight for it.

Claire Values?

The Boy Schoolgirls killed for going to school, mobs dancing on embassy roofs, burning books, what do you think would happen to you if you lived in Arabialand, Claire? Or Afghanistan? What do you think they do to lesbians? What's your general impression of the way little lesbian girls get treated in Islamic countries?

It's people like you who try to erase difference.

It's you people who won't call black 'black' and white 'white'.

Claire Pink – beige – sepia –

The Boy My daughter knows as many words in Polish as she does in English. In nursery they make her sing Polish songs. The kids make Polish food.

Claire I like Polish food.

The Boy Look, that boy – I don't even want to use his name – him – he's got nothing to do with us.

He came to some of our meetings. Once, I think I saw him at a disco. He was being a pain, hassling a girl. Some

of the lads threw him out. That's all. That's it. But now –
you should see the hate, the death threats – to me, to my
wife, to my daughter. I hate him. I despise him.

If I were running the country he would be dead now.

Claire Did you hate my choir?

The Boy No.

Claire You put it on a list.

The Boy I put it on a list of state-funded propaganda for
multiculturalism.

Claire You singled it out on your website.

The Boy Amongst many other organisations.

Claire My choir wasn't state-funded propaganda for
multiculturalism.

It *was* multiculturalism.

My choir was Jesse and Mr Aziz and Frank and Mrs
Singh and Isaac and Sherrie and Corrine and Gisela and
Kamal and . . .

That's who it was.

Was.

Now it's just me.

*

A solo Chorister sings 'A Song for an Imaginary Baby'.

Claire Look, a baby
    Newborn.
    Wet hair
    a pair of grey blue eyes.
    And such a pair of lungs.
    Look, a baby
    warm and damp . . .

grasping
searching blindly for a mother
for a breast to suck.
It's a boy.
I wind back time.
To the moment of his birth,
His mother holds him,
The nurse takes him out of the room to clean him.
I am the nurse.
I put my hand over his face.
I hold it there until he's limp.
Shh. I say. It's OK. It's OK. It's OK.
I bring him to his mother.
And his father.
Look, a baby
Still quiet
Cradled.
He must have been born dead
Poor thing, born dead.

It was a boy.

*

The Boy Where were you?

Claire I went up to The Den.

The bluebells are out.

Feels like spring.

The Boy How did it go with Dr Palmer?

Claire Interesting.

The Boy That's good. Isn't it? Is it good?

Claire It's good.

The Boy What did you talk about?

Claire The boy.

The Boy OK –

Claire He's not mad, Catriona. Not beyond the sense that he might be said to suffer from something we could call 'mass shooting event syndrome': a syndrome for which the primary indicative symptom is the planning and execution of a mass shooting event.

The Boy Right.

Claire He's actively had to suppress his emotions which proves he has emotions, so he's not psychopathic either –

The Boy Because I had thought –

Claire He *is*, however, odd.

The Boy That the idea of seeing Dr Palmer was –

Claire Odd but –

The Boy To help you sleep –

Claire He's not psychotic. His politics aren't deeply worn. His childhood was tough but not catastrophic. He did no paramilitary training, so whatever the reason it isn't *a* reason.

There has to be another way to explain it.

Something beyond –

The Boy Beyond?

Claire Beyond reason.

The Boy Right.
OK.
Did Dr Palmer say anything about you?
Did he maybe give you some pills, maybe some drugs?

Claire He did, but I threw them away.

The Boy Claire.

Claire It's hard enough to fight evil without fogging up my head as well.

The Boy Evil?

Claire Yes.

Evil is in the world, Catriona.

He brought it.

If I can find its cause and lay it to rest, I'll sleep.

Do you understand?

The Boy What if you can't find it?

What if bad things just happen?

What if even attempting to understand what happened to you is just a form of masochism: an endless throwing of yourself against a wall in the hope you'll break it down, which you won't, and if you ever did there'd only be another wall behind it . . .

What if shit just fucking happens?

Claire He's human.

If he's human I can connect with him –

The Boy Connect?

Claire Yes.

The Boy Claire, at this moment, you can't even connect with me.

And I'm trying.

I'm really trying.

*

The Choir join Claire in an improvisation.

Claire Tonight we're going to improvise.

I've been investigating shamanic practice.

And tonight, we're going to perform a ceremony to bring back our souls.

Because, you know, we've lost our souls,

Haven't we?

I've put a special herbal infusion in the urn.

This is a moment where the wise thing to do is to be unwise.

In a traditional society when you lose a soul – you recover it.

It's insane we don't know that.

And the person who does that is the shaman.

This is Dave.

Dave's from Leith.

Dave's going to help us bring back our souls.

So this is what we're going to do. Right?

First we're going to make a dream hut. Now we don't have an actual hut so we'll just use our bodies to form a circle.

Claire leads the Choir in clicking and humming.

We're going to make up the notes.

A simple chant – like this. What's the first thing that comes into your head?

Claire asks a Choir member. Whatever the response, however basic, she chants it. For example 'Er . . . um I don't know.'

You see?

'*Er . . . um . . . I don't know.*'
'*Er . . . um . . . I don't know.*'

   Claire claps, or stamps.

Everyone – keep going . . . We sing and sing and sing and drum.

   Claire leads Choir around the space, chanting. Boy follows using a traffic cone as a didgeridoo.

Now, bodied by your energy I will cross through the symbolic portal.

Form a symbolic portal!

Come on!

I step out of the earth world and into the world as dream.

And in that dream I quest

Down a path through woods

Rocks and the sea.

There is an island.

Fog on the water . . .

   Claire collapses.
     Silence.

Repetiteur I think maybe we should all break there for a cup of tea.

   The Choir collect tea from the urn

                        *

A member of the Choir becomes Mr(s) Sinclair.

Claire Mr(s) Sinclair?

I must have fainted.

Where is everyone?

Mr(s) Sinclair *They've gone.*

Claire Gone?

Mr(s) Sinclair *Home.*

Claire But we still have songs to work on.

Mr(s) Sinclair *I was given the job of speaking to you.*
We don't want to do choir any more.

Claire What?

Mr(s) Sinclair: *The things you've asked us to do lately.*
Shamanic ceremonies.
Aboriginal death chants.
Gaelic laments.
Lists of the dead.
Screaming.
They're not fun.

Claire Not fun?

Mr(s) Sinclair *They're depressing.*

Claire I'm trying to help us all heal.

Mr(s) Sinclair *Yes.*
But you do go on about it.
We liked singing pop songs.
And hymns.
We don't want to dwell on what happened.
We want to forget.
Perhaps forgetting is best.
Sorry.
Goodbye Claire.
Thank you for doing choir.

*

The Boy drinks tea.

The Boy This isn't really tea.

It's reindeer piss.

Today I attempt my first berserking.

He drinks.

I am watching a Bill Oddie DVD about foxes to try and observe the quiddity of their movement. I have taken a small quantity of fly agaric skin mixed with tea which I read on the Viking Warrior Shaman Forum was a good way to ingest the drug. I am sitting at the kitchen table. I have a washing up bowl beside me to catch the vomit. I am trying to stand outside the stream of my consciousness and note my thoughts –

Antiques Roadshow.
    Hate.
    The edges of things.
    Girls laughing.
    Smoke.

He falls asleep
    He wakes in a berserking state.
    He crawls around the room like a fox.

Claire I like to imagine him in that night.

A trial berserker,

An orphan in the moonlight,

Walking, singing, patrolling the bins by the coastal path,

Looking for a tribe to protect.

The Boy screams like a fox.
    The Boy vomits.

Claire Sometimes I wish we'd adopted him.

We always wanted kids.

Catriona and I, didn't we, Catriona?

In fact, it's the sweetest story

We love this story.

We were walking along the coastal path one day when we saw this lad – how old was he? How old would you say he was?

Fifteen. Let's say he was fifteen.

And he was sitting on a bin on the coastal path
    His knees up to his chin
    And he had an adorable face

We stopped and said 'Hello'.

He didn't say anything of course but we carried on chatting to him and it emerged his mum had jumped off a bridge and his dad was an alcoholic so we chatted with him, didn't we? And we must have been exactly what he needed in that moment because he followed us home and we invited him in.

'Come in!' we said. Didn't we?
    'Don't worry,' we said. 'We won't bite.
    Would you like to do some bird watching?
    Would you like some home-made bread?'
    And do you know he'd never had anything home-made before.

Anyway we adopted him, and now he's at Cambridge University

Studying law

He's at Strathclyde University studying technology.

He's at college.

He works in a shop.

A garage.

He's happy.

He's dead.

He died.

He's dead.

Claire I was thinking I might apply for a job.

The Boy A job?

Claire Chaplain – maybe.

The Boy Where?

Claire Peterhead.

East coast. Beaches. It would be great.

The Boy What sort of chaplain?

Claire Prison.

The Boy Somewhere?

Like where?

Claire Peterhead.

The Boy Peterhead Prison?

Claire Is that its name?

The Boy You can't sleep, Claire.

You can't eat.

What are you going to do in a high-security prison?

Claire It's important to turn dark things into light, Catriona.

The Boy In prison?

Claire Yes.

The Boy That's where he is, isn't it?

Claire No.
I don't know.
Maybe.

The Boy No. No. Enough, Claire. Just stop it.

Claire Stop what?

The Boy You have to stop this now. The tiniest piece of information you claw at it, anything, anything in the world that might give you insight into him you devour – but not me.

Claire You?

The Boy Yes.

Claire What have you got to do with it?

The Boy What have I got to do with it?

Claire You can come to Peterhead too.

The Boy Are you being sarcastic?

Claire You can make yurts anywhere.

The Boy I'm sick of this.

Claire Sick of what?

The Boy You. I'm sick of fucking you.

The Boy goes to leave, Claire pushes him.

Claire You can't leave me.

The Boy Why not?

Claire Because I'm the victim.

The Boy Just let me get past –

Claire I'm the victim here. You can't hurt me again.

The Boy Please don't stand in front of me.

Claire I'm not standing in front of you –

The Boy You're standing in front of me –

The Boy goes to leave, Claire attacks him.

The Boy Claire – get your – get off –

Claire Kiss me.

The Boy Claire

No.

Claire Just do it.

*The Boy pushes Claire off him. He goes to leave,
Claire attacks him.*

The Boy Claire, get off!

The fight is real, strained and slow.

Eventually Claire wins.

She spits on the Boy.
    She relaxes.
    She slumps.
    Exhausted.

Claire I'm sorry.

I'm so so sorry.

The Boy Jesus.

Why don't we both go away?
    Just the two of us.

I could learn how to make a bomb.

If we could just get up and go

To Somalia
    For guerrilla training.

To Iona
    For the festival of spirituality.

We could watch jihadi videos.

We could stay with the community there.
  You could pray,

I could manufacture a bomb with nails and bolts and stones bursting out the back of a rucksack tearing a hole through everything and everyone.

We could just do it.

What do you think?

Claire?

Because I'm running out of time

If I'm to leave a mark on the world I have to do it now.

*

Choir sing 'The Song of Gavrilo Princip'.

> *By the time he was my age Jesus had founded a new religion.*
> *By the time he was my age Bob Geldof had saved Africa.*
> *By the time he was my age Gavrilo Princip had fired the shot that started World War One.*
>
> *If I'm going to make a mark on the world I have to do it now!*

*

The Boy rocks on the balls of his feet.

Claire I see a boy – he rocks on the balls of his feet and since it's June and the evening's light and he's outlined against the red of the sun – back forward back – I wonder whether he's keeping to the rythym of our song.

47

And that's when he says.

The Boy Everyone who belongs here, go.

The rest of you are going to die.

Claire We're confused.

For all sorts of reasons we're confused

He's listening to music.

I can hear the tss-tss-tss of music bleeding from his headphones.

He moves smoothly.

The Boy Like dancing.

Claire Like dancing.

Is this real?
    Are we in a film?
    Why did Mr Aziz fall down?
    . . .
    Do I belong here?

I stare at him – bewildered.

I need to take control – I'm the person responsible – it's important for the safety of these people that I take control –

EVERYBODY RUN!

Claire Everybody run?

The Boy I can't help laughing.

Claire I mean, talk about stating the bleeding obvious.

The Boy Everything suddenly seems so – melodramatic.

Claire We scatter – panic –

The alarm goes.

The Boy Now noise – now sirens – now alarm and pandemonium!

It's strangely intoxicating this feeling of suddenly being at the centre of events.

Claire I run down the corridor to the music room. For no other reason than the music room is familiar. As I run I'm thinking – trying to understand – what's happening here?

The Boy Now, here's an interesting thing – I hope you don't mind – I think it sheds light; if you ever perpetrate a mass shooting event you are almost bound to spend at least some of the time during the event itself thinking –

This is silly.

Claire This is silly.

The Boy It's not that one isn't taking it seriously. It's just that when you're at the centre of events, you lose yourself. Except these strange, silly moments, these jolting eruptions of self-consciousness that interrupt your flow –

Like an actor drying.

Or a comedian forgetting the joke.

The Boy This really is very, very silly.

Claire I run – smash – batter – door after door – how many doors are there in this place?

I get to the music room –

Jam it shut!

Should I go back out?
    I should go back out.
    I should find others and bring them in here –

I put my hand on the door to go back out –

And that's I when see Mrs Singh.
   She's sitting in the corner.
   Her hands on her knees.

Mrs Singh is shivering.

Stay with me.

Claire Shh.

Shh.

It's OK. It's OK. It's OK.

The Boy I have one bullet left.
   Who is it for?
   Which one of you is it for?

*

Human beings are a species of ape. For a long time it was thought the apes to which we were most closely related were chimpanzees.

Like early humans, chimps travel in small bands, hunting and gathering. Chimpanzees are territorial. Groups are ruled by dominant males. If a group of chimpanzees encounter another group of chimpanzees in the forest they will fight each other to establish control of the territory.

Recently, in the Congo, a new species of ape was discovered, bonobos.

Bonobos also travel in small bands, hunting and gathering, but bonobos are not violent. Bonobo groups are ruled by senior females. If a group of bonobos encounter another group of bonobos in the forest, they will have sex with each other in order to establish relationships.

Humans share 98 per cent of our DNA with chimps.

And we share 98 per cent of our DNA with bonobos.
The other 2 per cent is just us.

*

Claire He kicks open the door.
　　And finds us.
　　He raises the gun
　　And in that moment.
　　I walk towards him.
　　I take his hand.
　　I kiss him,
　　I hold him,
　　I strip him.
　　I stroke him,
　　I take him into me.
　　I take him into me so gently,
　　And with so much tenderness and love
　　That he comes back to himself
　　His soul returns to his body
　　And at the exact moment he comes
　　I see it in his eyes
　　He understands
　　He understands that he is understood.

*

Claire What *are* you?

The Boy I am a Europe-wide malaise
　　I am a point on the continuum of contemporary
masculinity
　　I am an expression of failure in eroded working-class
communities
　　I am unique
　　I am typical

I am the way things are going
    I am the past.
    I am the product of the welfare state
    I am the end point of capitalism,
    I am an orphan
    A narcissist
    A psychopath
    I am a void into which you are drawn.
    I am sick.
    Dead.
    Lost.
    And alone.

I am a blankness out of which emerges only darkness and a question.

The only question it is possible to ask.

What is to be done with me?

Claire You will be taken from here and beaten with cable. Your body will be laid down on hot metal. The roof of your mouth will be gouged, the skin of your cock will be peeled, your feet will be burned, your muscles cut, shit will be smeared into your wounds, and the skin will be sewn up with septic string.

You will become sick and weak.

But on the point of death you will be cleaned, tended, healed.

And I will kneel by your head and whisper –

'Just outside that door is a meadow, a chalky meadow with buttercups, oak trees and soft grass. It is a wonderful place where you'll feel no pain and be enveloped in green and peace. It's just outside that door. So near. If you could just get there. If you could just crawl through that door, you would be free.'

And I'll open the door and I'll watch you as you pull
yourself forward on limp limbs and then just as you
reach the threshold,

I'll stamp on your neck and break your spine.

*

The Boy Hello.

Claire Hello.

The Boy Beautiful.

Claire Isn't it?

The Boy Admiring the view?

Claire Yes.

The Boy Stars and the moon and the sea.

Claire Silence.

The Boy Silence yes.

Claire Well, apart from the wind.

The Boy No traffic though.

Claire Yes, that's odd.
   It's normally very noisy here,
   The motorway traffic roaring.
   But tonight it's quiet.

The Boy All the traffic has stopped.

Claire Yes.

It's as if they did it for us.

The Boy They did.

They did do that for us.

They wanted it to be quiet so that I could talk to you.

Claire That's kind.

The Boy My name's Gary.
  What's your name?

Claire Claire.

The Boy Hello, Claire.

Claire Hello, Gary.

The Boy It's nice this, isn't it, Claire, you and me, sitting
up here in the warm breeze, looking at the sea and the
stars.

Talking.

Claire Yes.

The Boy Would you like to hold my hand?

Claire OK.

The Boy OK.

  Claire holds his hand.

Good.

I was just wondering, Claire,
  And you and me can talk as long as we like by the way
  But I was just wondering
  I was just wondering,
  If you would be willing to come away from the edge?
  Just step back over to this side of the parapet?
  Claire?

*

The choir speaks in unison.

Choir *Claire.*

  Why are you walking through The Den at night

Along the needle paths.

Claire gasps.

Claire I couldn't sleep.

Choir *Poor you.*

Claire I'm OK.

Choir *You must be cold.*
In your T-shirt and pants
And bare feet.

Claire Oh yes.
Ha ha. Embarassing.
I forget. I didn't expect to see anyone.
No. I'm OK. It's summer. I'm actually warm.

Choir *It's autumn.*

Claire Yes. It's autumn.

Choir *Why are you walking through The Den at night*
In your T-shirt and pants?

Claire Collecting mushrooms.

Choir *What sort of mushrooms do you collect?*

Claire Chanterelles, wood blewits, saffron milk caps,
penny bun.

Choir *Lovely names.*

Claire Lovely names.

Choir *What mushroom is that, Claire, the one that*
you're holding now?

Claire This one?

Choir *Yes. It's pretty.*
Is it edible?

Claire No, it's really really really poisonous.

Choir *What's it called?*

Claire Destroying angel.

Claire puts the mushroom in the teapot and swills it round.

*

Claire I forgive him.

I write letters. I contact chaplains and psychiatrists. I speak on radio programmes where I amaze people with my extraordinary capacity for

Forgiveness

I forgive him, I say.

He is forgiven.

I am on the news. I am on *Woman's Hour*. People share me on Facebook. People call me, 'the forgiveness lady'.

'How can you?' people say. 'How can you forgive him, after what he did, the beast.'

And I say. 'I can.'

I do it with love.

And they like that. They like it on Facebook and they like it in real life as well.

And so I wear them down, the psychiatrists and the chaplains, I wear them down with love and, in the end, they invite me to meet him and so one winter day I drive to Peterhead and they usher me through the gates, and down the corridor, and through the halls and into the special room they keep for meetings like this.

Hello, they say. Smiling at me. Amazed at me.

But in my pocket, I have a small amount of Destroying Angel which I have dried into a powder. A person would hardly notice it if they saw it. That's dust in a pocket, they would think if they saw it. But it isn't dust in a pocket.

It's poison.

And it will kill him.

It will erode his liver and it will kill him.

They will not like that on Facebook.

*

The Boy This is a nice room.

I've never been in this room before.

All gaily painted.

Look – they have an urn.

Do you want a cup of tea?

You could make a cup of tea.

I'm not allowed to make tea.

Do you want to make a cup of tea?

Claire No, thank you.

The Boy How was your journey?

It's been cold lately.

Did they do that thing when you came in?

Sometimes they do a thing –

They go 'Oooh oooh oooh', like chimps or something.

It's quite horrible.

Did they do that thing?

Claire No.

The Boy Well, that's something.

   He sits.

   Thank you for coming.

Claire Thank you for agreeing to see me

The Boy That's all right.

As soon as I got your letter, I was actually quite keen.

Claire Keen?

The Boy To meet.

My therapist said it might help.

My therapist says there's a thing.

Sometimes if you meet the people you hurt.

If you meet them and say sorry.

It helps.

Claire Do you need help?

The Boy I have trouble sleeping.

Claire I didn't know that.

The Boy I hardly sleep at all –

Claire Since the events?

The Boy Since I was a kid –

Always.

I used to use dope, drink . . . you know.

Self-medicate.

But I'm not allowed that in here so –

My therapist said meeting you might help bring closure.

Claire Have you met any of the others?

The Boy Others?

Claire The other people you hurt.

The Boy Oh. Them. No.

Claire Only me.

The Boy None of the other people would come.

Claire Some of them are dead.

The Boy Even the not-dead ones wouldn't come.

Claire Perhaps the not-dead ones don't want you to sleep.

The Boy No, it can't be that . . . I don't think . . . I mean, that wouldn't make sense.

Claire Wouldn't it?

The Boy They don't know about my sleeping problems, do they?

Claire No.

The Boy My therapist said I should meet you.

He said you would want to ask questions.

He said I should answer every question honestly.

Claire There's only one question I want to ask.

The Boy Fire away.

Claire Why?

The Boy Honestly?

Claire Honestly.

The Boy I was angry.

Claire Plenty of people are angry.

The Boy I was angry and I had a gun.

Claire Why?

The Boy This was all in the papers.

Claire Why?

The Boy I don't really remember. Someone told me about a man in Leeds who had a gun. I had the idea I should have a gun, so I went to Leeds and I got it.

Claire Why?

The Boy Honestly?

Claire Honestly.

The Boy There was a girl.

Claire You didn't mention a girl at the trial.

The Boy Didn't I?

Claire No.

The Boy I forget sometimes what I mentioned and what I didn't mention.

Claire I was at the trial every day and you didn't mention a girl.

The Boy One night a silver car stopped outside my house.

The back door opened and a girl fell out on to the pavement.

It was getting dark so I couldn't quite see. There were three men in the car all dressed in white. The girl was in a red miniskirt. I couldn't really see. The driver got out of the car and he hit her. He was wearing one of those white shirt things – I don't know what you call them. He slapped her face. The car's engine was really smooth, you know. Silent. He hit her again. The other guys in the car watched. The girls on the chippy wall watched. Then the man got back in the car and they went away.

After an hour she was still there.

I said – 'Hello,

You look like you've been crying.

Are you all right?'

That sort of thing.

And she smiled.

So then I said, 'Do you like *Call of Duty*?'

And she nodded so I said –

'Would you like to play *Call of Duty* with me?'

We mostly played the two-player game.

Then she fell asleep on the sofa.

I put my sleeping bag over her.

The sunlight was coming in off the sea, bugging me, making the screen bleachy. I think I had a headache.

I looked at her, lying there on the sofa –

All soft, like water or something –

And I thought –

What I need, is a gun.

Claire To kill her?

The Boy To protect her.

Claire Why?

The Boy Honestly?

Claire Honestly.

The Boy Honestly?

I think I just got a bit obsessed with aborigines.

. . .

Look – Claire –

I feel a bit sick.

My mouth's all dry.

I'm very sorry about this.

It happens.

If I talk – I get – discombobulated.

I'm really sorry.

Claire No, it's OK.

Claire goes to the urn.

Do you want some tea?

I'll be mother.

Claire makes a cup of tea from the urn.

You know the boy,

The aboriginal boy.

The one you wrote about standing on the rocks, the sails on the water.

Do you remember?

The Boy Yes.

Claire I often wonder, when you imagined him.

Did you ever imagine asking him how he felt about those ships?

What he thought?

I mean only wonder because . . .

Isn't it possible, isn't it just possible that – after sixty thousand years of entirely unchanged culture – isn't it just possible that if you asked the aboriginal boy how he felt about seeing those ships in that moment he might say – in an aboriginal language of course – something like 'Thank fuck! Thank fuck something interesting has finally happened round here.'

That's possible, isn't it?

The Boy It's possible.

Claire puts a cup of tea in front of the Boy.

Claire When you came into the music room.

I was in there with Mrs Singh.

Do you remember?

The Boy Not really.

Claire And you pointed the gun at us and you said,

'I have one bullet.

Which one of you do you want me to shoot?'

Do you remember?

The Boy I remember, yeah, yeah,

They said in the trial, I said that.

I remember it now.

Claire 'Which one of you do you want me to shoot?'

That's what you said.

The Boy Yeah.

Claire Why?

The Boy Honestly?

Claire Honestly.

The Boy I was tired.

I had one bullet left.

By that point, I was thinking the whole thing was – silly.

I just wanted it all to be over.

Claire Do you remember what we said?

The Boy No.

Claire We both said 'Me'.

> *The Boy reaches for his cup of tea.*
> *Claire knocks the cup of tea off the table, it spills.*

The Boy What did you do that for?

＊

Caretaker Claire.

Claire You must be the new caretaker?

Caretaker Yes.

Claire How many chairs do you think I should I put out?

I put a notice up on the board.

It said 'Choir's Back On, As Before'.

So people know, don't they?'

But still.

Some nights there's something on the telly.

Do you think it's worth putting chairs out?

Do you think anybody will come?

Caretaker I think
You'll be all right.
People will come.

The Choir sing: 'We're all here'.

Choir *Outside it's dark*
  Outside it's raining but
  In here there is warm
  And people, everyone, the rehab man,
  And young mums from the centre,
  Waheed and Isaac, and Agnessa too,
  Some people from the church,
  The service users
  And we're all here, we're all in here

  Sometimes Chantal and Kai just wander in
  And Simon brings his sister
  And people, everyone, the Polish crew,
  The young man with the temper
  Ex-offenders
  And we're all here, we're all in here.

Claire welcomes the Choir.

Claire Come in.
  Don't be shy.
  Everyone's welcome here.

We're all one big crazy tribe here.

If you feel like singing – sing
  And if you don't feel like singing
  Well that's OK too.
  Nobody feels like singing all the time.

Choir (*sing*) *And we're all here, we're all in here.*

  The End.